About thi

This book is a summary of many year
some glimpses into the lives and hom
centuries.

The following people who have studied aspects of Wymondham's history, have helped in building up the picture – Philip Yaxley, John Wilson, Brenda Garrard, John Ayton, Richard & Minn Fowle, Sheila Spicer and Judy Hawkins. Many of those who live in the street now, or did so in the past, have generously helped in the search for the history of their houses. Some former residents of Damgate have kindly shared their memories and are mentioned in the text. The Town Archive managed by Janet Smith and Mary Garner, has provided an invaluable resource over many years, as have the collections at Wymondham Heritage Museum. We also acknowledge the help and advice of George R Reeve.

In arranging the material in the book, we begin at number 1 on the east side and go along to Damgate Bridge. There, we cross over to number 70 on the west side and work back to number 2. We hope this arrangement will be convenient for those who wish to walk Damgate and also those who just want to read about it.

Some historical background

Damgate is one of the most historic and important streets in Wymondham; the gateway to the town from the west. For centuries it was the main highway to Norwich from Thetford, Cambridge and London, until the 20th century by-passes were built.

Damgate may have got its name as the road leading to the dam of the water mill. From the Domesday Survey in 1086 AD, we know that before and after the Norman Conquest, there were at least two (water) mills and a fishery in Wymondham.

From the earliest times, houses were built along this street. Today, their facades conceal historic features of great age and interest.

Some Wymondham families with Damgate links

Throughout the centuries, some of Wymondham's best known families have either lived in Damgate or owned property there, the most famous perhaps, being the Ketts.

In 1417, Richard Kett, an alderman and great grandfather of Robert Kett the rebel leader, lived in Damgate. Thomas Childerhouse and William Kett (Robert's brother), had three cottages in a row in 1534-5 in the Abbey Manor. James Kett, one of Robert's sons, also had a cottage in Damgate in 1546.

In 1578, John Kett, grandson of Robert gave up 'the orteyard wall, formerly the monasterys' and 'a piece of ground formerly the Abbey garden' to his mother Agnes. In 1585 Agnes allowed her son William, grandson of Robert, to use a property called 'breeses' and the 'orteyard wall in Damgate and a piece of a great garden formerly the monasterys.' William died in 1614, 'dwelling in Damgate.' Many of the properties on the west (Abbey) side of Damgate had documents referring to the Abbey wall and lands.

In the 19th century several Ketts, mostly weavers, lived in the Alligator's and Chalker's Yards of Damgate, including George Kett the great, great, great, great, great, great grandson of Thomas Kett, younger brother of the rebel leader. The 1881 census reveals that Eve Kett was the town librarian – the library and reading room was located in the Market Cross.

From c. 1500 – 1650 many of Wymondham's wealthiest and most influential families lived in or had property in the street. Robert Chaplin, a member of many religious gilds, left bequests to them and the Abbey when he died in 1500. Documentary sources suggest he may have lived very near numbers 49-53, Damgate. William Rowse, a brewer, also had a 'mansion house' in the street in the 16th century.

In later centuries, among the many prominent families who had property in Damgate, were the Baileys, Aytons, Crannesses, Bowgens, Whartons, Canns, Harveys, Crosses and Panks.

Victorian Damgate

The census returns reveal a great diversity of occupations among the residents of the street in Victorian times. Unskilled and semi-skilled workers, rubbed shoulders with apprentices and tradesmen; innkeepers jostled with craftsmen like wood turners, cabinet makers, tailors and printers (the aristocracy of labour), as well as painters, glaziers, plumbers, an engine driver, and a marine engineer. There were many shopkeepers, including, butchers, bakers, drapers, grocers, ironmongers and green grocers. In 1891 there were 14 dressmakers living in the street and 17 residents in service. The people of Damgate were the 'nuts and bolts' of the local community. Their skills and labour serviced the town, local gentry and the more comfortably off in the neighbourhood. It was truly a working man's street.

By the 1880s most residents were married with children. All the men worked unless they were very elderly. Housewives were bringing up children and most single women also worked. The 1881 census reveals a society in transition. Weaving, wood turning, harness making and leather cutting were in decline, but small businesses were appearing, railways were making an impact and state education had arrived. The growth of brush making and brewing are reflected in the 1891 census, industries which would overhaul boot and shoe making as major employers in the town. By then, there were 14 residents employed in brush making and nine working on the railway.

The occupations of Damgate residents illustrate many of the new developments in the late Victorian world such as schooling, nursing, railways, postal services commercial traveling, newspapers, libraries and factory work. The street was a microcosm of Victorian Norfolk, a vanished world of close knit families and older relatives living together; a respectable hardworking community grappling with significant social and economic forces which would transform their lives.

At the time of the 1891 census, of the 335 people living in Damgate, three quarters were Wymondham born. There were 81 families and 91 children. Some 208 adults were working, just under a third of whom were artisans.

Some 20th century changes

Many of the changes which have occurred in the 20th century have been referred to in the book. Despite continued commercial vitality, there has been a decline in the number of shops; the cluster at the Market Street end is a far cry from the golden age of shops in Damgate. That century saw the disappearance of Chalker's and Alligator's Yards and the building of the old people's bungalows.

The greatest benefit to Damgate residents of course, was the first by-pass and more recently the coming of the one way system in 1995. Today, properties are largely private houses, enjoying the benefits of quieter times. The residents must be grateful it is no longer the main gateway to the town.

A common sight in Damgate before the by pass

Centuries of habitation and architectural evolution have left their marks on the street. Contemporary sale signs, renovation, and alterations are modern reminders of what have always been a feature of Damgate houses and people – adaptation and development.

George R Reeve Ltd
Corner of Damgate & Market Street

Before George Reeve took over these premises as a shop and printing works, Clarke & Co general store, occupied this spot which was known as 'Clarke's Corner.'

Clarke's was founded by Edward Clarke in 1881 and Harry Clarke took over about 1920. The shop continued until his death in 1969. Alice Keep, an evacuee, still recalls being registered there for food rations during the Second World War. Harry Clarke was known for his cheerfulness and served on the Urban District Council.

The Seager family now run the friendly gift, greetings cards and stationery shop as well as the printing works on Town Green, contributing greatly to community life in the town.

The corner of Damgate and Market Street in the 1940s

Number 1 Damgate

This is now a private house but in the past it has been used by various businesses. Before the 1970s it had been at one time a cobbler's shop. Above the entry on the left, was the workshop. It had no staircase and was reached by a ladder. There was also a glass panel in the dividing wall to the bedroom where the cobbler's wife could communicate with her husband!

In the 1970s it became 'Cottage Things' selling wooden and iron quality objects, toys and kitchen equipment - one of the first of such shops which are now common in the area. The Damgate Bookshop (now the Book Fountain in Wharton's Court) followed, and also a Men's Casual Clothing shop and a Cake Decorating shop.

Numbers 3 & 5 Damgate

Number 5 was once the home of Mr & Mrs Elkins. Mr Elkins was a prominent member of the town's Fire Brigade and the National Fire Service during World War Two. Mrs Elkins ran a pram and toy shop where the Market Street Travel Agent is now. Mr Elkins' father, was a noted photographer who had a shop in Market Street.

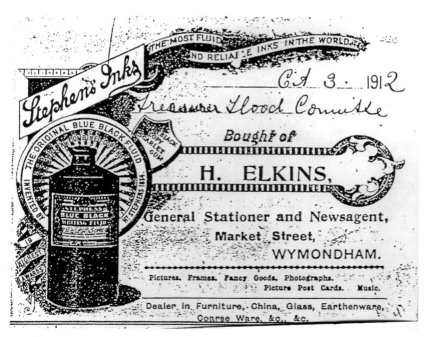

THE MOST FLUID AND RELIABLE INKS IN THE WORLD.

Stephens Inks

THE ORIGINAL BLUE BLACK FLUID

C.A. 3. 1912

Treasurer Flood Committee

Bought of

H. ELKINS,

General Stationer and Newsagent,

Market Street,

WYMONDHAM.

Pictures, Frames, Fancy Goods, Photographs.
Picture Post Cards. Music.

Dealer in Furniture, China, Glass, Earthenware,
Coarse Ware, &c., &c.

Numbers 7 & 7A Damgate
(now a Chinese restaurant & takeway)

Alfred Harvey (1910-1985), was one of the great Wymondham characters. In these premises he ran Alf's fish and chip shop from 1935. He also had a van for Wymondham and the surrounding villages. He was one of Jesse Harvey's 16 children and was born at number 63 Damgate. His daughter Sheila (now Mrs Eaglen), remembers her father telling her that his father Jesse, who was a tailor, would sit crossed-legged in the former shop window of number 63, sewing.

Alf and his wife outside their fish & chip shop

During the Second World War at Christmas 1943, American servicemen distributed sweets with names like 'Neccos' and 'Lifesavers' from Alf's shop, to 300 youngsters from local junior schools.

Children queuing up for sweets given to them by the Americans at Christmas time 1943

Sometimes Alf would dress up in his pearly king outfit. He was a Norwich City mascot during City's F.A. cup run in 1958-9. He would walk around at Carrow Road, holding a large cut-out canary.

Number 9 Damgate

This was formerly a jeweller's shop run by Mr R Cooper who would go around the large properties like Kimberley Hall and Stanfield to wind and care for their clocks. The Coopers had a beautiful garden at the back. Later the business was taken over by another jeweller Mr W Hawkins. In recent years the premises have been used as a Gun shop and as Ebony furniture and bric a brac shop.

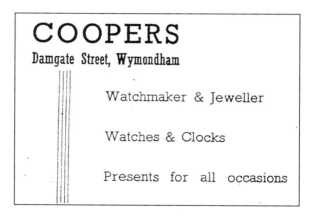

COOPERS

Damgate Street, Wymondham

Watchmaker & Jeweller

Watches & Clocks

Presents for all occasions

Number 11 Damgate

Now a private house, this was a greengrocer's shop before the Second World War, run by Mr & Mrs Slaughter. Ian Slaughter moved here when he was nine. When he left school he worked at Briton Brush and the CWS Brushworks.

He joined the RAF in World WarTwo, but when he came home in 1945, his parents had moved but had forgotten to tell him!

Eventually he discovered they were living in Bridewell Street – he recognised the curtains!

Ian's uncle and aunt bought number 59, Damgate. His aunt ran a sweet shop there while his uncle worked at Briton Brush.

Number 13 Damgate

The house when it was Michael's Hair Fashions in the 1990s

This Grade II listed house is built of 18th century brick with a pantile roof. Timber framing to the south side indicates an earlier structure. A central arch leads to a passage to the rear. There are two tall gabled windows at the back of the house. Inside on the ground floor is a chamfered bridging beam. A recent owner carrying out renovation, reported fire scorching in the roof timbers and old bottles were also found there.

Some 18th century owners:
1712 John & Elizabeth Proctor sold the house to Richard Barton, a weaver for £42. 3s.
1722 Elizabeth Barton (widow), sold it to Thomas Dersley, a bricklayer. He was responsible for building the Infirmary on the Lizard in 1766.

No. 13 in recent times:
For 24 years the property was Michael's Hair Fashions, but it is now a private house. Before 1978 it was empty for over four years. Previous occupants, the Ex- Servicemen's Club, built a large flat roofed extension to the rear. From about 1925 it was a 'Penny Lending Library' and a sweet shop and tobacconist run by James Felstead. His widow, Mrs Ethel Felstead took over and had a franchise for all the Sunday papers in Wymondham, which she sold on to others.

12

Mrs Felstead at her shop door

Number 15 Damgate

This property is now an antique shop.

Numbers 17 and 19 Damgate

These properties are not listed and are private houses.

Numbers 21 and 23 Damgate

Now one property, these houses are late 18th century rendered and colour-washed brick, with pantiled roofs. They were at one time the offices of the local Labour Party and formerly Cawdrons and Barwells wine merchants.

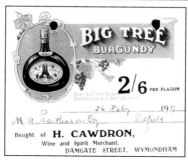

Numbers 25 and 27 Damgate

A pair of apparently, early 19th century houses of brick, with pantiled roofs

Numbers 29 and 31 Damgate

Originally two houses and now one, this property was once the Gildhall of All Saints Gild. It is the only gildhall in Wymondham to be identified so far. The gild's account book records the old building being taken down and the 'newe house' built. An entry in the manor court roll of Norton from 1534, describes it as 39 feet high, 30 feet wide and 44 feet in depth from the road.

There were many religious gilds in Wymondham which were established for mutual support in medieval times. They were dedicated to particular patrons (in this case All Saints), ensured proper burials for members, prayed for their souls and gave grants in times of hardship. Officials were elected and membership was open to all, including women. Gilds also acquired property to rent and had their own gildhall to celebrate their annual feasts.

In 1512 the old house was taken down and the new one built and reed-thatched. Thomas Dowsing was responsible for taking out the old timber, while Newman of Thorpe assembled the new timber frame on the ground sill, already fixed by William Bale. It took Richard Alden ten days to reed-thatch the house. John Colyour the tenant and gild member, lived in part of the building, which he eventually purchased. Other work was carried out on the well, gates, stable, stairs, hearth and oven and Robert Grond and his servant constructed a pentis (outhouse) on one side.

Numbers 33 and 35 Damgate

These houses are the first two in a terrace of four which appear to date from the 19th century. Number 33 is on the old street line and shares a continuous gabled roof with number 35. Its front has been rebuilt in brick with the roof raised and has a 'flying freehold' to the south, its bedroom being over number 35's ground floor bathroom. Its chimney is mid 16th century added to an earlier building, which seems to have been an open hall dating from the mid 15th century.

Inside on the right hand side of the brick inglenook fireplace, are some pieces of dressed stone with diagonal cuts. These, as in other houses in the town, could have come from the Abbey which was dissolved in 1539.

On an interior wall, originally outside, is a plaster panel with 16th century APOTROPAIC marks, in the form of daisy wheels or 'witch marks' to protect the house from fire or evil.

At the 1806 Enclosure, Robert and Ann Edwards claimed both of these cottages. Robert was a glove maker. During the 19th century, Damgate became a focus of the leather working trade.

Numbers 33 and 35

The daisy wheels or 'witch marks' on an interior wall of number 33

Numbers 37 and 39 Damgate

Both these houses have inglenook fireplaces, winder staircases and timber framing.

Number 39 still has part of its flint façade and was once the Half Moon Inn, one of the town's many lost pubs! William Pudding kept it in 1708. At the time of the Enclosure Act 1806, it was owned by William Cann the Wymondham brewer, but it does not appear in the Directories after 1836. In 1885 it was described as 'the messuage called the Half Moon.'

Number 41 Damgate

The building

The red brick exterior of this house with its plaque of Queen Victoria, conceals a cosy cottage of great age. The front door leads directly into a room with a very large inglenook fireplace with the original winder staircase to the right. There is a chamfered bridging beam to the wall opposite the fireplace. This wall has a flint plinth with a massive beam resting on it, supporting the exposed timbers in the wall.

A very wide 18th century doorway with original door leads from the front room to the former rear stable. The back wall in which this door sits has a secret – it was once the outside wall before the lean-to kitchen was added. An original window of great age and in excellent condition has been revealed, with a section of wattle and daub walling beneath.

The rear stable has now been incorporated into the house and there are two staircases. Upstairs are more exposed timbers and a Victorian fireplace. A house of surprises!

Some occupants

In 1871 Sam Leamon, a shoemaker, was living in the cottage and legend has it that he used to take his horse through the front room to the stable, followed by his wife with a bucket and shovel! In 1934 Charles Robert Ayton, who was the owner of the Wymondham stone pits, sold it to Mr Bunn the baker for £200.

Exposed window and remains of wattle and daub in the sitting room wall

Number 43 Damgate

This property belonging to the Manor of Choseleys, has documents dating back to the 17th century.

Some 18th century owners were John Nickless of Tasburgh, a flour merchant and Thomas Nickless a hairdresser of London. In 1793 Samuel Staff, a baker, bought it and a baking office, yard, garden and outhouse and also three other cottages.

By 1879, this house and number 41 next door, had been rebuilt, the other cottages demolished and the new Wesleyan Chapel and school room erected next door. In 1893, number 43 was bought by Samuel Carman of Wymondham. At some later date, the side extension was built and from the late 1920s a greengrocery was run there by Mr Dent and then Mr Burgess. In the 1970s it was a Thrift shop and then a graphic designer's. It is now a private house.

The Masonic Hall
(between numbers 43 and 49)

This was formerly the Wesleyan Methodist Church and was opened in September 1879 when the Rev. Josiah E Whydale of Whitby, preached two sermons.

It was constructed of brick with stone facings for 250 persons with a schoolroom, coach house and stable for visiting preachers. A gallery runs around the inside and the cast iron railings with tulip finials at the road side, are also listed. The total cost of the site and building was about £900 and the builder was a Mr Ketteringham. Those who contributed included Mrs Gunns,

£60, Miss Eva Rayson, who had owned the site, £60, JJ Colman MP, £10, Sir FGM Boileau, Bart. £10, CS Read MP, £2, Harry Bullard, Mayor of Norwich, £5, EHH Combe, Mayor of Yarmouth 2 guineas, John Gurney, £5, Henry Birkbeck, £5, RT Gurdon, 3 guineas, Col GM Boileau, £2 and William G Fryer, of Browick Hall, £2.

Among the trustees were William Rayson, father-in-law of the builder and Samuel Carman, town official and gentleman who bought number 43.

In 1932 the Primitive, United and Wesleyan Methodists amalgamated and 22 members from the Damgate chapel moved to Town Green. The sale of the Damgate chapel for use as a Masonic Hall, was finalised in 1935.

Numbers 49 – 53 Damgate
- known as the 'three in one'

From one to three and back to one again!

This property was at one time sub-divided into three parts, but is now one house again. It was originally timber-framed front and back, with a flint and brick cellar and various recesses under part of the rear range. It has been subject to many alterations from the late 17th century and has an under built jetty. It may have been truncated by half a bay when the adjoining properties were demolished to build the chapel.

In the ground floor sitting room (originally number 53), there is a chamfered beam. A large fireplace with niches has been revealed with a winder staircase to the right. A wattle and daub wall divides the sitting room from the rear service room of what was once number 53. This room has a flint wall.

In the present dining room (formerly numbers 49 & 51), there is another exposed fireplace with the initials S.G. carved on the bressumer, possibly those of Samuel Galliard the owner in 1710. This beam also has scorch marks from candles. The room has oak panelling which has come from Aldermaston Hall.

Inglenook fireplace in the lounge

A Tudor archway leads to the breakfast room and from there, another arch leads to the present kitchen. This was originally outside with a pump beneath the floor which served seven cottages which ran at right angles from the property (see sale details on page 24). The end wall of one of these cottages, now forms the outside wall of the present kitchen.

Timber framing with blocked in and re-sited windows upstairs

Upstairs there is extensive timber-framing with blocked windows to the rear. In the main bedroom a Victorian fireplace has been un-blocked and restored. Another staircase to the right leads to the attic.

The house's 18th century owners included John Kett, a spindle maker. His executor, Samuel Weavers, was a spoon maker. Its present owners have undertaken a massive restoration project on this historic property.

In the lovely rear garden of the property, the present owners dug up a red Commer van which had been cut into pieces. They also found a quantity of leather waste – Damgate was a centre for shoe-making in the 19th century. A large number of oyster shells were also found.

When the property was three houses c. 1960s

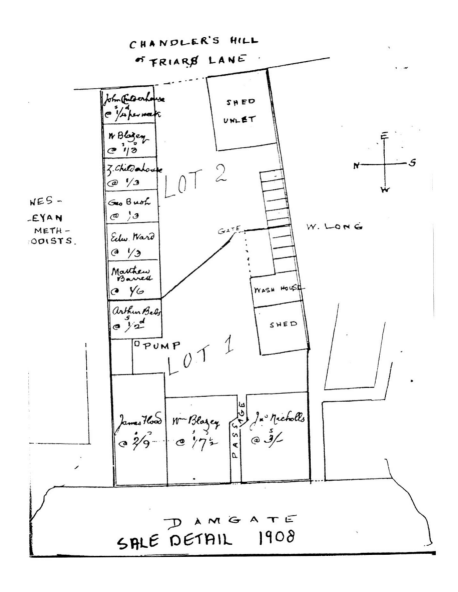

Plan showing numbers 49, 51 and 53 as separate properties

The 'three in one' today

Numbers 53A and 55 Damgate
formerly Corston's Stores

William Henry Corston opened his shop in 1919 on returning from the war. There was an alley way through to Chandler's Hill and the shop was bought from Mr 'Bunky' Wells.

When the family went to clean the shop they found 12s 6d on the floor! The first week's takings were 19s (less than a £1). Mr Corston had to go out to work until the takings improved while Mrs Corston ran the shop. In the 1920s they bought the property next door and opened a drapery where they sold a range of clothing, including 'long johns' and corsets; the shop van was kept in Alligator's Yard opposite

The Corston's two shops

In the 1970s when their customers were moving to the new housing estates in north Wymondham, the shop moved with them! The drapery closed first and was used for a time by Mrs Corston (William Henry's daughter-in-law), for EC Business Services. When the grocery closed, Mr William Corston opened a store in Lime Tree Avenue and Hubert Corston ran Town Green Stores. Their sister Mrs Bedingfield, ran a drapery store in Town Green which is now Middletons.

She had also worked for her father and weighed up sugar, flour, lard and currants. The currants came from Greece and were cleaned in a machine operated by turning a crank. Once through the cleaner, they were sold at 6d per pound and twice through the price rose to 8d, but in each case the currants were wrapped in blue paper.

About the building:

Number 53A is a house of the late 17th century or earlier. A third storey was added in the late 19th century. The roof is glazed black pantiles and there is a rendered plat band and dentil-eaved cornice, as on numbers 50-56, opposite. Next door, number 55 also dates back to the 17th century.

Mr William Corston remembers:

When his father took over the Damgate shop, many odds and ends had been left behind. He obtained some smallish paper bags and put in a mixture of shirt buttons, pins and chest-rub 'cure-alls', selling them at the shop door for 2d to the workers who passed by after finishing work at the Briton Brush factory in Whitehorse Street.

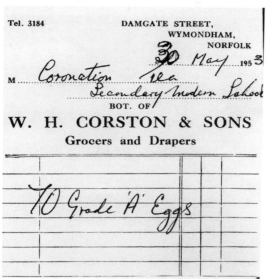

Tel. 3184

DAMGATE STREET,
WYMONDHAM,
NORFOLK

30 May 1953

M Coronation Tea
Secondary Modern School

BOT. OF

W. H. CORSTON & SONS

Grocers and Drapers

10 Grade 'A' Eggs

Before the business acquired a van, they would cycle to Suton and Spooner Row to collect orders and then deliver them again on trade bikes with the basket on the front. Lorries would deliver goods like soda to the door in sacks; the bags were carried in, weighed and bagged up, then sold at 1 penny a pound.

Like others, Mr Corston remembers cows being kept in the yard behind numbers 29 and 31 and a Scotsman in full Highland dress doing a sword dance outside the 'Two Brewers' at number 30.

The Corston family has been traced back to 1765. The noted Wymondham mineral water manufacturers are related, as Hubert and William's grandfather and Wesley and Jonathan Corston's grandfather (mineral water producers), were cousins.

Number 57 Damgate

The 18th century panelled door and white-washed brick front, give few clues about what lies within.

The living room has chamfered beams and a large inglenook fireplace with massive mantle beam. There is a winder staircase to the left and a recess to the right. Substantial steps lead to the elevated rear kitchen through an 18th century doorway. The inside wall of the kitchen has what appears to be an outside window. This wall continues into the recess mentioned above, where it has

another concealed window. Upstairs is much exposed timber work and a very high ceiling. It is believed that this was formerly one large room.

Number 59 Damgate

Now a private house, it is pictured here in the 1950s with CT. Slaughter General Stores over the door. Mr Slaughter took over the shop in 1932 and was still serving in 1973 aged 86.

The shop front with its Victorian wrought iron decoration has been recorded by English Heritage. There was a Regal Cinema poster to the left of the door.

The house dates from the 17th century at least. A 17th century shoe found in the house is in the keeping of Wymondham Heritage Museum and the inglenook fireplace in the dining room, has been dated to 1670 by a Norwich Castle Museum archaeologist.

At the rear of the house is brick tumbling on the gable similar to that on number 50 opposite. Some of the guttering is of great age and a well has been converted into a water feature.

Below are adverts from the Grocer's Gazette of 10 June 1939, which were found in the house.

Numbers 61 and 63 Damgate

Numbers 61 and 63 are a pair of houses with a shop front, now residential only. They appear to be 18th century and of brick with a pantile roof. They are pictured here in the mid 20th century.

Numbers 61 and 63 are near right

However the cottages were believed to have been the Lion's Head inn during earlier times and in 1708, John and Mary Rose owned them.

Mr Jesse Harvey Senior

Jesse Harvey (1863-1914) a tailor and father of 16 children lived here. Jesse was also the town crier, an office he inherited from his father Robert Harvey, described in 1881 as 'bellman'. Later his own son Jesse took over as town crier and tolls collector of open spaces. He served for 31 years until his resignation in 1945.

In 1893 Salter & Simpson sold by auction, *'a red brick and tile double tenement. Part 1 – sitting room, tailors shop, storeroom and three bedrooms occupied by Jesse Harvey and Part 2 – sitting room, kitchen, storeroom and three bedrooms occupied by Charles Watts. Also a small piece of garden ground with outbuildings, corner of Damgate and Friarscroft, let at £13 p.a., property of Philip Bowgen, of the manor Choseleys.'*

Ancient Order of Foresters
Court "BUD OF HOPE"
JUVENILE SOCIETY

Registered under the Friendly Societies Acts

Objects— (a) Sickness Benefit.
(b) Funeral Benefit.   (c) Medical Benefit.
Parents should insure their children in above Society, as Boys and Girls are now admitted between the ages of 1 and 16 years.
Funds invested over £200.

For particulars and entry forms apply to

**JESSE HARVEY, Secretary,
Damgate Street, Wymondham**

Number 63 is entered straight from the street. The door has an original security bar across it. There is an inglenook fireplace and a winder staircase still in use; exposed timber framing can be seen throughout. The doorway to the kitchen has an original door with a small glass panel so that customers could be seen from there as they entered.

This property has been owned by well known Wymondham families, including the Bowgens, Crannesses and the Bunns. In 1973, the cottages were sold separately.

Number 65 Damgate – The Sun Inn

Formerly the Sun Inn, the property is now a private house. The 17th century north range has a shaped gable added in 1720. A south extension was added in the late 18th century and an east one in the late 19th century. The early north range is thatched and the rest pantiled. The early north range has a chamfered bridging beam to the ground floor and a wide open fireplace in the east wall, with a winder staircase to the east side. A date-stone in the south gable could be 1792 or 1795.

DAMGATE AND SUN INN (WITH RARE FLEMISH GABLE). WYMONDHAM.

Some owners and publicans at the Sun Inn

1756   Edward Amond took over. He was one of the Sun's most famous proprietors. In 1783, he became governor of the Wymondham Bridewell. A Lowestoft mug dated 1768 with a sun and inscription 'Edwd Amond Wymondham', is in Norwich Castle Museum.

In the 19th century, The Sun belonged to the brewers Cann & Clarke. There were lovely pleasure gardens going down to the Tiffey.

1806   At the Wymondham Inclosure:
        'John Stephenson Cann claimed the messuage, tenement or public house called the Sun, with garden and appurtenances thereunto.'

Some other licensees:

1836	Rising Sun	Wm Smith
1845	Rising Sun	William Smith
1864	The Sun	Jno Foulsham
1868- 71	Sun Inn	Ambrose P Harper, builder
1883	Victualler, Sun Inn & bowling green	John Lain
1916	Sun	Harry Fennell

Other activities at the Sun Inn:

In 1739-40 the Post Office was run there by Michael Hobbs. Later on, auctions were held on the premises and at one of these, on 4 June 1858, George Barnard a weaver, bought three cottages, gardens and land occupied by James Corston and Jonathan Doubleday for £120.

The Sun Bowling Club was very active and in December 1924, Mr Pomeroy, a local solicitor, was invited to attend a smoking concert. There was a large hall behind the Sun where Mrs King of Damgate had her wedding reception. Mr & Mrs Davidson also ran a tea shop at the property at one time.
The Sun Inn closed in 1958.

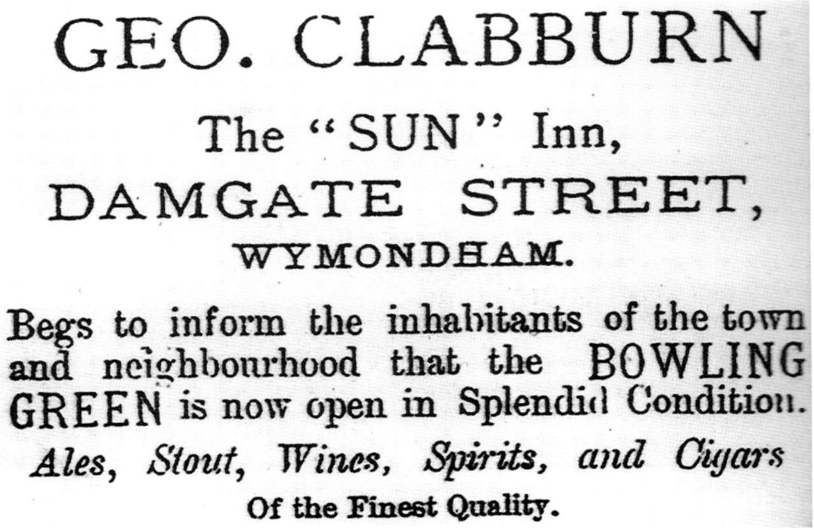

GEO. CLABBURN

The "SUN" Inn,

DAMGATE STREET,

WYMONDHAM.

Begs to inform the inhabitants of the town and neighbourhood that the **BOWLING GREEN** is now open in Splendid Condition.

Ales, Stout, Wines, Spirits, and Cigars

Of the Finest Quality.

The Sun Inn Bowling Club 1919

Back row: l to r: W Walker, G Kidd, J Corbould, T Brown, E Blyth, E Glanford, 'Shaver' Kerrison, T Walker.
Seated, l to r: W Carter, F Hadingham, 'Tumbler' Smith, E Blyth (Snr), A Tyler.
On ground: W Carter (jnr), J Harvey.

Ian Slaughter's memories:

'I was born in 1923 in the cottage behind the Sun Inn. From a small window at the top, I could see into the bar. Times were hard then, but they were happy days and we had great fun running in and out of the alleyways between Damgate and Chandler's Hill. The many children in Damgate in the 1920s were always playing out. Every year Corston's Grocers would have a party at the back of their shop (number 55), where between 50-100 children would sit at long tables.

Where the Chandler's Hill housing development is now, was once a large vegetable garden and orchard owned by the Crannesses, who lived in Victoria Villa.'

Number 67 Damgate – Ostler's Cottage

This property has had two other names – 'Riverside' around the 1900s and 'Sun Cottage.' It was once two cottages which were knocked into one, the oldest part being the flint section nearest the river. There is a keystone on the chimney with the date 1602 and the initials R.T. Sun House, formerly the Sun Inn has the date 1603 and the same initials.

The interior has been altered - the inglenook and bressumer have been removed and reduced in size and staircases have been changed. The kitchen is late Victorian/Edwardian and was formed from a flint wall with eight extra brick courses on top and a roof. A bathroom was also added on. The timbers supporting the roof are quite rough, with bark on some. Despite the many changes the cottage retains many charming and intriguing features.

Sketch of Ostler's Cottage, near right

The Dam Bridge

The bridge may take its name from the dam for the water mill nearby. Important roads from Thetford, Cambridge and London crossed the river Tiffey here. The bridge would have been a very stable feature of the landscape; the earliest structure was made of wood and stone and in constant need of repair.

The Wymondham 'Town Book' records payment of 26/- in 1613 for 100 feet of planks and in 1616, 10/- was paid to *'carpenders and other workmen for amending of Damm Bridge against the Judges coming over yt, the stoune being much decayed'*.

In 1616, 16/- was paid to *'the diverse pore men that laboured to quenche the fyer happened at Damm Bridge and for watchinge the same all the next night for the safety of the Towne'*. The Great Fire of Wymondham in 1615 would have been a recent memory and the townsfolk were being particularly careful to prevent another.

In 1618 the bridge needed attention again when 3/4d was paid to Stephen Agas for repairs. Agas was one of the Headboroughs or Constables for the Damgate division of Wymondham.

Damgate bridge from a drawing by Francis Stone in 1830

Floods and more repairs to Damgate Bridge

In August 1696, Robert Nixon of Wymondham was paid 10 shillings for providing his horse and cart and four labourers to dig, carry and lay gravel on Damgate Bridge before it was broken down by a great flood. After the flood, another £1. 6s was paid to him for faggots and gravel and eight men to get up the timber carried away by the flood and do other repairs.

In April 1756, the General Quarter Sessions held at Norwich Castle, agreed to pay *'Mr Johosaphat Postle 8s. 2d in full, for repairs to Wymondham Mill Dambridge.'*

On 26 August 1912, flooding destroyed the Hubbard and Nicholls' family homes which adjoined the bridge. After this flood part of a millstone was found near the bridge. The Wymondham Flood Relief Fund paid compensation to these Damgate residents for their losses:

Robert Smith, labourer, rent 3s 0d a week.
>Losses: 1 fork, 2 slashers, 1 spade, box of tools, wood, crops in border, valued at £1. 8s

R Elliott, GER labourer, rent 3s 3d a week
>Losses: 6 cwt coal, 2 buckets coke, 2 baths, garden tools and matting, valued at £1. 5s

Charles Coggle, wood turner, rent 4s. 0d a week
>Losses: coconut matting, clothes, books, damaged furniture and wall paper, 2 cwt potatoes, valued at £4. 10s

Charles Butcher, fish hawker, rent 3s. 0d a week
>Losses valued at £1. 2s 6d.

Numbers 70 – 64 Damgate

These four houses are believed to have originally been one large merchant's house which could date from the late 15th or early 16th century, with later additions and alterations.

They have a continuous roofline along the whole range and the steepness of the roof suggests they could have been thatched and jettied.

Number 72 before it was demolished

Number 70 Damgate

This property was constructed of flint and brick with an attractive crow-stepped gable to the south. When numbers 70 and 72 were purchased in 1979, a restoration programme was begun and number 72 was demolished.

Like many early houses, number 70 was resting on a flint plinth with tile on the top. By the 17th century, plinths were usually built of brick or a mixture of flint and brick.

Inside, the house has magnificent deep, full-moulded ceiling timbers which may have come from the Abbey. It has been suggested that it was once the Abbey Chamberlain's house.

Number 68 Damgate

This house is also part of the terrace (numbers 70-64) thought to have been one house. The front wall is now brick-faced and was originally jettied.

Inside, there is a flint wall and also a cob wall – unusual in the area. The main bridging beam is a continuation of the one in number 70. In the back wall a mullioned window was exposed. In the bedroom there is evidence of former blocked mullioned windows in the front and back walls. During renovation, some wattle and daub was uncovered in an attic wall.

Number 66 Damgate

This property has one of several fine stone fireplaces in the town, possibly from dressed stone from the Abbey remains. Its intricately shaped chimney of yellow brick, is 16th century.

Number 64 Damgate

This house is timber-framed with some oak beams of great age, which are exposed internally. The exterior exposed timbers are decorative and recent additions. There is a former carriage entrance which led to the rear. During alterations, horse brasses were discovered, suggesting evidence of former stables. Between numbers 64 and 66, there was once a through passage which is now bricked up.

There are three chimney stacks from different periods. The oldest is of twin flue construction and early. In the roof void, which is now the second floor accommodation, the timber framed structure is exposed. A structural frame of re-used, possibly Tudor timber, was inserted more recently during renovations. A dividing wall and other structures separate number 64 from 66, where part of number 64 extends at first floor level over number 66.

Numbers 66 and 64

These two houses were occupied in 1810, by Jacob Kett, a descendant of Thomas Kett, brother of the rebel Robert. He married Mary Fickling of Damgate in 1801. Their children were Jacob, Susannah and Elizabeth Frances Kett, a schoolmistress who did not marry.

The property was sold in 1885 for £235, to James Cranness, a joiner with a beer house in Fairland Street and Charles Harrison, a carrier who conveyed goods to Norwich on Mondays, Wednesdays, Thursdays and Saturdays.

Numbers 64-66 remained one house 'Belitha' until 1980 when number 66 was sold separately.

Numbers 62 and 60 Damgate

These houses (near left), of colour-washed brick, date from the 17th century or earlier and have a saw-toothed cornice. There is a passage way between the two to the rear. Inside number 62, a striking feature is the moulded bressumer, over a magnificent brick inglenook fireplace with several niches. A staircase was originally to the right of the inglenook. A massive chamfered beam runs from front to back like the one in number 64 next door.

Number 58 Damgate

This property was formerly a shop. The private house today is colour-washed brick with a pantile roof and a dentil and saw-toothed eaves cornice. It was altered in the early 19th century, the central shop door being flanked with two bow windows used for display. Inside there is a chamfered bridging beam on the ground floor and some plain chamfered joists on the first floor.

This is a view of the back entrance to number 58 and the three storey weaver's shed in Alligator's Yard, which runs from the street just downhill of the old people's bungalows and goes behind numbers 50 – 56. The traces of the end of one of the weaver's cottages that occupied the west side of the yard, can be seen on the wall of the weaver's shed.

Weaving in Wymondham

In the mid 18th century, weaving was the chief occupation in Wymondham. The 1782-8 Easter Offering Records, lists 31 weavers in Damgate alone. According to the 1841 census, there were 79 silk and worsted weavers (and one other) in Wymondham. But by 1845, the number had dropped to 60.

Number 58 and weaving

This picture shows the weaver's shed and cottages in Alligator's Yard, now demolished. A beautiful garden belonging to number 58, now runs behind numbers 58-70 and down to the river, where there are peaceful views of the Abbey and meadows.

In 1765 Samuel Harvey, a glover and skin dealer, inherited number 58 on the death of his father Francis. When Samuel died in 1816, his son William Harvey, described as a worsted weaver and bombazine (fabric) manufacturer, inherited the property. However, before his death Samuel had mortgaged the property to Francis West of Norwich and in 1824, West reclaimed the house.

The weaving syndicate

In turn, West sold the property in 1824 to a 'weaving syndicate' which included William Harvey and was headed by Samuel Bignold, son of Thomas Bignold, founder of Norwich Union. Samuel Bignold was mayor of Norwich four times and founded the Norwich Yarn Company in 1833. He lived in what is now the Norwich Union Fire Office in Surrey Street. Whether the weaver's shed was purpose-built or converted from the premises which Samuel used for his skin business, is not certain.

However, the 1810 Wymondham Enclosure map shows substantial structures behind number 58 in Alligator's Yard.

Weaving is phased out

Between 1824 and 1873-4, when the property was sold to William Clarke a grocer, the weaving was phased out. William Harvey had disappeared from the property by 1851 and various tenants took over. Several of the tenants of the adjoining cottages were still described at this time, as handloom weavers. A John Noble, coach builder, was there at the time of the 1861 census. The weaver's shed was finally demolished in 1973-4.

Number 58 becomes a shop

At J.H. Hall's shop in 1879, you could buy 1 lb of sausages for 10d (less than 5p today), half 1lb of butter for 7d, 7lb of sugar for 2s (10p), 1lb coffee for 1s 8d (less than 10p) and 2 pints of Canary seed for 5d.

J.H. Hall, butcher & general provision dealer, outside his shop in the late 19th century

Memories of Mrs King of Damgate

Mrs L King who was born at number 50, remembers number 58 as a butcher's shop run by the Hall family. Behind it was the slaughter house. Her father Frederick Mabbutt and Mr Hudson, would help when the pigs were killed. The pigs would be put in a tub and all their bristles scrubbed off. Sometimes, after a pig's bladder was cleaned out, children would use it as a balloon! When Mr Colman took over the business, it became more of a grocer's shop.

Since then, number 58 has been an Antique Booksellers (John Ellis 1958-73), Photographers and Engravers, (Mr & Mrs Davidson 1973-6) and an Antique Dealers (Mr & Mrs Dixon 1976-8).

The property has been a private house since 1978.

ESTABLISHED OVER 60 YEARS

FRANK HALL,

(Proprietress, L. HALL)

Butcher and
General Provision Dealer

Damgate Street
WYMONDHAM

Our Noted Sausages Fresh Daily

Numbers 62 to 50

Numbers 56 to 50 Damgate

These properties form a terrace of colour-washed brick houses with a plat band at the first floor, (see drawing on page 46) and pilaster strips framing the terrace. The houses possibly date from the 17th century or earlier. Numbers 54 and 56 are now one property. There is a magnificent brick inglenook fireplace with a small cupboard and winder staircase to the right of it and substantial chamfered ceiling beams. Superb oak doors from the former Briton Brush factory, now link the two living rooms.

The owners of numbers 54 and 56 have created a lovely garden with beautiful views, from the site of the demolished weavers' cottages. There is an original flint wall on the left, part of the sty, where the pigs were kept (see Mrs King's memories).

The rear of numbers 54 & 56, with the sty on the left

The original 'privies' remain at this property, together with a large drain where tin baths and washing water were emptied in earlier times.

Between 1964 and 1987, Mr & Mrs Lane lived at number 56. There was a damp patch on the wall adjoining number 58. They were told that it was caused by the salt used in curing hams. The cottages that were in the yard behind number 56 (Alligator's Yard), were quite small and a Mrs Colman lived there. When they were pulled down, the site was sold as a garden to the owner of number 54.

Number 50 Damgate and George Mabbutt

George Mabbutt was born at number 50. He worked for 48 years at the Briton Brush Company, retiring as Quality Control Inspector. He was a town councillor and vice chairman of the Urban District Council. He and his wife fostered children and he ran a junior football team and a youth club at the United Reformed Church. He was a school manager, a member of Toc H, the Royal British Legion and later secretary of the Over 60s club.

In 1996 he was presented with Maundy Money in recognition of his great contribution to the life of the town. His sister, Mrs King, still lives in Damgate.

Damgate's Yards

In this part of Damgate, there were three yards – Hubbard's Yard behind numbers 49-53 and 55, Alligator's Yard and Chalker's Yard.

Alligator's Yard runs downhill from the old people's bungalows and behind numbers 50 to 56. Seven houses were included in a sale notice of around 1900 viz: *the yard with outbuildings, gardens, pump and well of water at rents amounting to £34 9s 2d p.a. Mr J. H. Hall had the right to pass over Alligator's yard to Damgate.* Next door, Chalker's Yard (now demolished and the site of the old people's bungalows), had eight brick, stud and tiled houses, outbuildings, gardens, pump and well. The rents were £34 17s 8d pa.

These yards existed at the time of the 1841 census and from then until 1871, a number of wool, silk and cotton weavers lived there including, George & Maria Kett, John & Sarah Dover, the Blazeys (4) and the Peels. After 1871 numbers of weavers dwindled. How Alligator's Yard got its name is a mystery, but there may be a clue in that Samuel Harvey was a fellmonger and skin dealer (alligator's skins?). John Chalker of Chalker's Yard certainly existed as did John Hubbard.

Damgate's links with the Charge of the Light Brigade, 1854

1274 Sgt John Howes

Sgt John Howes was a survivor of the Charge of the Light Brigade on 25 October 1854, during which he was slightly wounded.

Howes was born in August 1828 to Elizabeth Howes and Dives Blazey, who married in 1829. John was baptised on 6 July 1829. Both his parents were weavers and appear on the 1861 census living in Alligator's Yard, Damgate.

In 1846, aged 18, Howes enlisted in the Light Dragoons, using his mother's maiden name. In 1853, he was promoted sergeant and served in the Crimean War for nearly two years. He was awarded the Crimean medal with clasps for Alma, Balaclava, Inkerman and Sebastopol, the main battles in the war and also the Turkish medal.

In the famous charge, Cornet George Warwick Hunt called up Sgt Howes when he reached the Russian guns, to help him carry one of them away. They tried to release the gun, but were unsuccessful and Lord George Paget their CO, told them to remount. Howes was on a difficult horse, not his own, and received a cut to the side of his head from a Russian hussar. Eventually he reached the safety of the British lines, claiming to be the last man to do so.

On 11 October 1857, Howes became Troop Sgt Major. After he was discharged from the Army while in Dublin in 1860, he moved to Birmingham where he became one of the most respected former soldiers in that city. At the age of 73, he was in the Guard of Honour at a banquet to commemorate the return of Joseph Chamberlain from South Africa in 1891, when they shook hands.
In 1875 he attended the first Balaclava banquet. During Queen Victoria's golden jubilee in 1887, he signed the loyal address. He died in 1902 and was buried with military honours in Lodge Hill cemetery, Birmingham

Sgt Howes in full uniform

1036 Private Richard Bunn

Born in 1818, Richard, son of Thomas Bunn a Damgate weaver and Mary Bowhill, was baptised in the Abbey Church on 12 April 1818. In 1839, he enlisted in the 4th Light Dragoons (4th Hussars). He became batman to Lt. Henry Astley Sparke, who went missing during the Charge of the Light Brigade. Bunn may also have ridden in the charge.

Canon and Mrs Sparke, parents of Lt Sparke, received a letter from the injured Bunn, whose return to his Norfolk home was delayed by a spell in hospital in Chatham. He was discharged from there and moved to Mile End Road, London on 22 January 1856. He did not take a place at the Royal Hospital, Chelsea in 1857 and died in Bethnal Green on 19 November 1860.

Mrs King remembers Chalker's Yard

'In Chalker's Yard, next door to us, were four old cottages. Three of them had three storeys and there was a fish shop run by Mr Smith. Next to the yard was a hairdresser's run by Mrs Childerhouse and a wooden hut where Adelaide Cross had a wool shop. When the road was icy, we would put ashes down to help the traffic up the hill.'

**Houses in Chalkers Yard –
now the site of the old people's bungalows**

Photograph by John Ayton

MRS. M. CHILDERHOUSE
Hillbro' House, Damgate,
WYMONDHAM.

HIGH-CLASS LADIES' & CHILDREN'S HAIRDRESSING

Marcel Waving.   **Setting.**   **Water Waving.**

BY APPOINTMENT.

1934

Damgate's links with the Chartist movement

During the great depression of the 1830s which caused much hardship and discontent among the poor, some of the residents of Alligator's and Chalker's Yards, became drawn to the Chartist movement, which campaigned to improve the lot of the poor.

In 1838 the Peoples's Charter was drawn up demanding political reform, including votes for all male adults and secret voting. It also sought social and economic reforms to improve conditions for the working classes.

John Dover, a Chartist from Chalker's Yard

Dover and other Wymondham Chartists, arranged for a Chartist speaker to come to the town in 1839. Dover issued handbills about the meeting which was to be in the Market Place. However, the authorities got to hear about the plan and broke up the meeting, though the speaker did return later to talk to Chartist sympathizers.

The Church of the Latter Day Saints (Mormons)

In the 1861 census, the Church of the Latter Day Saints is recorded as being next to Alligator's and Chalker's Yards.

In the 1851 census of Religious Worship, there is mention of a preaching room with seating for 100. On 31 March 1851, 70 attended service in the afternoon and 43 in the evening. Robert Dye, a master bootmaker, was the 'residing elder' of this branch of the church. The population of Wymondham at this time was 5,177.

Robert Dye was ordained minister in the Mormon Church and in 1858, he and his family emigrated to Salt Lake City in America. Other local residents, including Hyrum Reeve, followed. Reeve attained high office in the Mormon Church and his house in Salt Lake City, is said to be still in use and a smaller one next door has the name 'Wymondham' carved over the door.

Numbers 36, 34, and 32 Damgate

On 1 December 1972, these houses were sold by auction at Central Hall Wymondham, by W.S. Hall & Palmer. They were described as an end of terrace and two terraced cottages, with mainly brick and partly flint elevations under tiled roofs

From the left, numbers 36 to 26

A listed building schedule described them as early 19th century brick with pantiled roofs. However, a conveyance dated 13 April 1671, confirms that number 32 has a much earlier core. This document declares:

> 'to all Christian people to who this present writing shall come, that John Scrooke of Walsingham, apothecary, son and heir of the late John Scrooke of Wymondham, conveys to George Kett:
> All that messuage with the appurtenances situate, lying and being in Wymondham between the highway on the east part and the wall of the late abbot and convent of Wymondham on the west part and abutting on the messuage late of Christopher Scott towards the north and the messuage late of Jonathan Brewer towards the south.'

On the early 19th century map of the lands of the Rev Papillon, vicar of Wymondham, the properties appear to be in the ownership of M. Stone.

Number 30 Damgate – The Two Brewers

This house has an early 19th century colour-washed brick façade on a much older building.

In 1659 Benedict Browne owned the property and his mother Mary lived there. Ann Bush took over when Mary died and in the 18th century, the house became the public house, 'The Two Brewers' which incorporated a greengrocer's shop. The property belonged to W.R. Cann the brewer, in the 19th century.

In his book 'Wymondham Inns', Philip Yaxley relates the tale of the local wag who drove a bullock into the pub for a laugh. It had to be raised from the cellar with a tripod and ropes!

Mrs King who lived at number 50, remembers men smoking clay pipes there in the early 20th century. More recently the house was called 'Gondri' or 'gone dry'.

Numbers 28 and 26 Damgate

These two houses with early 19th century brick skins, were owned by William Stamp and his wife in 1660. In 1680, Stamp a tailor, left both houses in his will, to his wife. After her death his son John Stamp was to have *'the house where I now live'* (number 28) and his daughter the house where she lived (number 26) *'with the two chambers and the yard thereto belonging, with a well to draw and take water.'* His son John Stamp *'shall have the privilege of the yard belonging to his sister to hang and dry white lyning and also to the well to draw and take water.'*

John was left *'40s of good and lawful English money,'* and *'all my wearing apparel'*. Elizabeth Fenn, his sister got £5.

After his wife's death Elizabeth also got one warming pan, four skillets, a pewter chamber pot, two stools, one iron dripping pan and one spoon. John got the rest of his 'goods' and his books were to be divided between his two children.

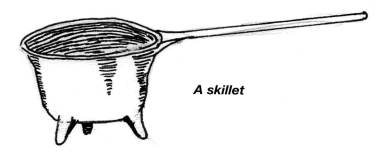

A skillet

More about number 28

In the 1806 Enclosure, Ann wife of Cooper Leatherdale, claims, *'a cottage and schoolroom, with the yard and garden in the occupation of James Parker, copyhold of the Manor of Wymondham the Queen.'*

In 1842 the bottom of the present garden was bought from the estate of the Rev William Papillon. Similar plots were sold to other Damgate residents at this time. In the same year, John Smith bought number 28 from Stephen and Mary Standforth and James and Hannah Cooper. In 1860 John Smith bought number 26 too – the properties were then in joint ownership until 1965.

More about number 26

In 1806 at the Enclosure Act, Mary, wife of Grime Carter claims, *'a cottage, yard and garden in the occupation of John Faulkes, copyhold of the Manor of Wymondham the Queen.'* In 1826, the Rev Papillon bought the property. After Papillon's death, his coachman Jeremiah Friar and his wife Letitia were given a lifetime lease.

Some Damgate residents and the Swing Riots of 1830-31

The 'Swing Riots' is the name given to the unrest and agitation among agricultural workers in 1830-31. Many were victims of trade depressions which led to wage reductions. They were also hit by the new threshing machines which reduced jobs. The 'Swing' activities involved attacks on threshing machines and the burning of corn ricks. Rioters often left a threatening letter signed by a 'Captain Swing' in an attempt to get justice from the farmers.

During this unrest, three Wymondham men, John Smith, Stephen Jackson and Tom Wells were arrested and sent to Norwich gaol. Eventually only Wells was found guilty of arson. Thomas Leatherdale a witness, gave this account on oath, of what he saw:

'I was at Robert Rix's farm at Wattlefield where stacks and other property were destroyed on 19th November. I saw John Smith walking towards Park Farm (adjoins Rix's farm) on the previous evening, and he was half a mile from his home in Damgate.'

John Smith said that he was at home in Damgate from 3 o'clock and there was a meeting, planned the previous Monday, of about 30 people at his house between 6 and 9 pm. They read acts of parliament and documents about the overseers of the poor and church wardens. They had also talked about a petition to the government.

Stephen Jackson said he had been to the Dove public house at the Town Green end of Pople Street and then gone on to Smith's house.

Tom Wells said he had meat and beer at Smith's house.

The following Damgate men whose family names appear on the census, were also at Smith's house:

William Bunn, Robert Harvey, Heron Howes, John Howes, Lazarus Blazey, Jonathan Blyth, Isaac Smith, John Jacobs, John Bayley, James Nixon, Robert Livock, William Drake, Thomas Foster, Samuel Butler, John Tuttle, Barnabas Lincoln, Richard Kett, Stephen Plunkett, Richard Peel, Robert Reeve and James Fiddymant.

Number 24 Damgate – Jetty House

The Jetty House has a late 18th century brick façade concealing an earlier core. It has a flint plinth course, often a sign of a pre- 17th century building. It is mentioned in the Queen's Manor Court Book of 1769.

Notes on Wymondham Breweries, in the Town Archive, call it a 'Bower House' – that is, a place where the owner could sell alcohol on Fair Days, without having a licence.

During a recent restoration, a tiny window was exposed (top left of the façade) and above the Regency door case, there may be another.

The present house could have once been two buildings with one room per floor, each with its own stack and staircase. Alternatively, it could have been one house with the north part used for business and the south for the owner's private accommodation. In 1810, it was owned by Jacob Lucas, a baker, so the latter idea is a possibility. Lucas sold the house for £220 to Zaccheus Reynolds in the same year.

Numbers 22 & 20 Damgate – Harvey House

The core of this property is a late 15th century hall house, much altered and added to. It is partly timber-framed with late 18th century brick facades and additions.

Harvey House was once a beer house belonging to the Harvey family, local brewers in the 18th century. Bottles found in the cellar can be seen in the Heritage Museum's brewery display. It was later acquired by Cann & Clarke's brewery.

Inside, the front door leads to a passage with an inner doorway with early 17th century features. The south ground floor room has chamfered beams; there is a winder staircase to the west of the chimney stack. A timber four-centred arch (now blocked), is set in the east wall of the hall range.

Harvey House is near left

In the early 19th century plan of the Rev. Papillon's lands, the owners are shown as Harvey. William Harvey brewer, is claiming several premises and a large amount of land at the time of the 1806 Enclosure, but none can be identified as Harvey House.

A surveyor's report on Harvey House in 1954, said it was probably Tudor and had a heavy oak frame with lath and plaster. The brick work probably dates to the 1830s.

Another business carried on in this house was that of antiques. A 1912 bill head of George Cross, dealer in antique and modern furniture, boasted that the business was established in the reign of George III (1760-1820).

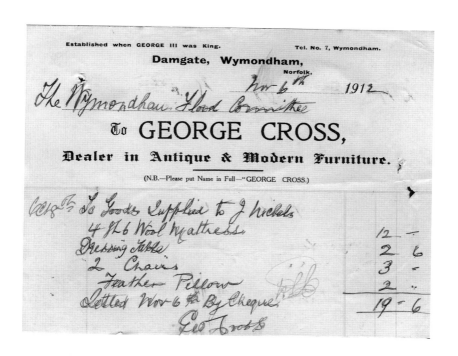

Nov 6th 1912

The Wymondham Flood Committee

To GEORGE CROSS,

Dealer in Antique & Modern Furniture.

(N.B.—Please put Name in Full—"GEORGE CROSS.)

Oct 18th To Goods Supplied to J. Nichols			
4 lb 6 Wool Mattress	12	-
Dressing Table	2	6
2 Chairs	3	-
Feather Pillow	2	..
Settled Nov 6th By Cheque	19	6

Geo Cross

Some prices of goods added to stock in 1916. In April of that year the value of the stock in hand was £621 1s 0d.

Chippendale round table	2. 5. 0
2 Elbo chairs (painted)	18. 0
Mah.Hanging wardrobe	2 10.0
Palm stand	1 0. 0
3 Chippendale walnut chairs	4. 0. 0
Walnut wine cooler	2 10.0

Goods in Stock Jan. 1st 1908

Mahogany Bookcase
Mahogany Chest drawers
Jacobean Chest drawers
Walnut tall Boy
Tall Boy
692 Elbos Mah: Chairs
Walnut chest drawers
5ft side board
Inlaid Jacobean chest cabinet 4 draws
Small Mah; wash stand
Mah Bureau
Wheat Ear Bed Poster
Ditto
Ditto
8 day clock Oak case
Gate Leg table Oak small

A page from George Cross's stock book

George Cross's daughter Vita, who had been a nurse at the Red Cross hospital at Abbotsford, in Vicar Street, during the First World War, took over the shop in due course.

Vita Cross outside the shop

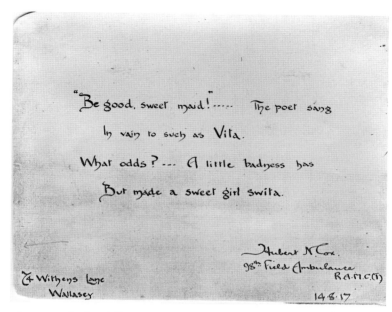

"Be good, sweet maid!"..... The poet sang

In vain to such as Vita.

What odds? --- A little badness has

But made a sweet girl swita.

Hubert N Cox.
98th Field Ambulance
R.A.M.C.(T)

4 Withens Lane
Wallasey

14·8·17

*A wounded soldier convalescing in Abbotsford Red Cross
Hospital in 1917, wrote this appreciative poem about
Nurse Vita Cross*

Information about the Cross family kindly provided by Mrs J. Bunn.

In due course, Leslie Fiske had his barber's shop in the front of the house. His son Cyril has described the gas ring under the ornate urn that heated the shaving water and how the News Chronicle, was cut up for lather papers, after it had been read! At a later date, Mr Watson also had a hairdressing business on the premises.

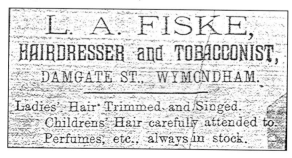

L. A. FISKE,
HAIRDRESSER and TOBACCONIST,
DAMGATE ST., WYMONDHAM.
Ladies' Hair Trimmed and Singed.
Childrens' Hair carefully attended to.
Perfumes, etc., always in stock.

Number 18 Damgate – Oak House

Numbers 24 to 16, Oak House 3rd from left

This property dates from the 15th century, with later additions. It is colour-washed and timber-framed. The central 16th century door is plank and stud. The first floor is jettied.

The rear of the house and the two storey hall range, are timber-framed. There is a former loading or 'suicide' door to the first floor and the interior has much exposed stud work, some wattle and daub and oak and hazel staves.

In the past this house served as an inn, known as 'The Duke', 'The Duke's Head' or even 'The Duke of Cumberland.'

In 1866, a Benjamin Weston was caught stealing 17 pints of beer at 3 am. He was arrested by P.C. Hook, who had  hidden in the hayloft at the rear of the building. This story was researched by Philip Yaxley.

The inn closed in 1906 and became a private house. In 1953 it was sold for £230 to the tenant, Sidney Victor Clarke. In the 1970s, the property was beautifully restored as a restaurant, but later reverted to a private house.

Some licensees of the Duke's Head

1836	William Cranness
1845	William Cranness
1864	Thomas Mayger
1868	James Wilsom
1871	James Wills
1881	William Smith
1883	William Oakley

View of the Abbey behind Number 18

Number 16 Damgate

This property has been both a private house and a shop. It is partly timber-framed but now mainly colour-washed brick.

In 1890 John Robert Wharton founded his butcher's shop here. The sheep and cattle tiles can still be seen beneath what was the shop window. Wharton's sold home-bred meat from the Earl of Kimberley's estate, which was slaughtered at the rear of the shop. In 1938 the business expanded to Town Green and Market Street. When the Market Street shop closed, the family business had been in the town for 100 years. Peter Wharton still carried on the traditions of courtesy and service with the old-style sawdust on the floor, together with chopping and preparation blocks. It is greatly missed by all his former customers.

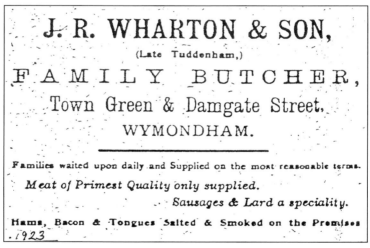

Robert Wharton married Elizabeth Bush and they had three children, Ella, Tom (Peter's father) and the youngest Eva, born in 1907. She married George Howard Chapman. Their children are Philip and Elizabeth (Portsmouth).

More meat was sold from the Damgate shop than any other. It is now a private house, but has also been a saddler's and for a time the home of Adlard's Restaurant.

Number 14 Damgate

This private house dates from the 17th century or earlier and is colour-washed brick and partly timber-framed at the rear. There is a carriage entrance to the north. Inside is a large chamfered bridging beam to the ground floor. The property was once occupied by Home & Commercial Security.

Numbers 12 and 10 Damgate

These properties may date from the 17th century. Various florists have run their businesses from number 10, which has also been a bridal shop and Moroney's solicitors. Number 12 is a private house.

Tom Turner, the Town Clerk, was buying these bouquets for use at the time of the celebrations for the Coronation of Queen Elizabeth II.

Numbers 14 to 6

Number 8 Damgate

This property dates from at least the 17th century and has housed a variety of businesses.

It was once the Abbey Gift Shop and Tea Room, run by Mrs Leighton and Mrs Ann Smith in the 1970s. It later became a branch office of Eastern Counties Newspapers and is now Badgers Antiques

Number 6 Damgate

Adelaide Cross lived here. She had a lock-up wooden wool shop near to the present old people's bungalows in Damgate, and later a shop in Market Street.

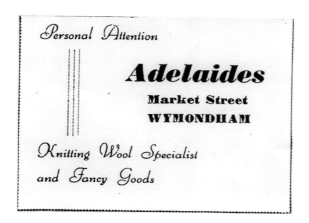

Personal Attention

Adelaides

Market Street
WYMONDHAM

Knitting Wool Specialist
and Fancy Goods

She worked hard to set up the present Roman Catholic Church in the town and her father carved the altar in this church.

Number 4 Damgate

This property has housed a variety of businesses in the past. Howes & Son Ironmongers and Cycles, can be seen in the photograph on page 68. The premises have also sold fabrics, been a toy shop and a pine furniture store. Until recently it was Light Works and is now Ebony.

The Abbey Gift shop, number 8 and Howes & Son Ironmonger and Cycle shop, number 4 in the 1960s

The rear of Howes' Ironmongers shop.

The Rose & Crown, Damgate

Formerly the Rose & Crown tavern, (2nd from left above), this building is wholly timber-framed with a carved jetty bressumer. In 1739 it was re-named Lord Rodney's head after the famous admiral. In 1794 it reverted to its old name and finally closed in 1911. The building has been used as an antique shop, the Lemon Tree Café and is now Crème Cafe.

The carved jetty pictured left, has mouldings which could date from 1480-1530.

Some licensees of the Rose and Crown

1836	Charles Brown
1845	Jonathan Sany
1864-71	Robert Welton
1876	W Robert Bowgen
1881	Charlotte Welton
1883	Thomas Mays Amis

Proctor's Shoe Shop

There is a long tradition of boot and shoemakers living and working in Damgate. The footwear shop of A.G. Proctor & Son, is the oldest family retail business still trading in the town. It started in 1914, when Arthur Proctor, with £3 to his name and help from his parents, began selling boots and shoes and doing repairs in Bridewell Street.

In 1930 he moved to the shop at the corner of Damgate and Church Street. He was told by George Reeve the printer, that he would fail, because people always walked on the other side of the road and would not cross! At first, everything was hand sewn – Arthur Proctor even made his own thread from six or seven strands of hemp.

During the Second World War, Colin Proctor remembers that everything was rationed and you needed the right number of clothing coupons to buy an item. Wellington boots were in such short supply that you had to have official permits too. Yellow permits were issued to firemen, the police and ARP wardens; blue permits were given to others who could prove

Arthur Proctor at work

they needed them. Footwear could not be sold without the correct coupons and permits.

The retail price of 'Gents' rubber boots then, was 29s. per pair. Colin Proctor took over the shop when Arthur died and he liked a 'bit of snow', because it helped to sell Wellingtons! This popular, friendly and valued business is still in the Proctor family.

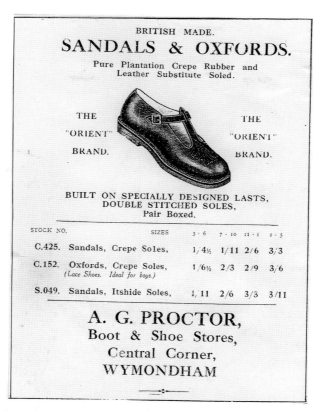
About the building occupied by Proctor's shoe shop

Proctor's shop occupies a 16th century building which is timber-framed and brick. It was formerly the Goat public house. It is believed to be the building referred to in this entry in 1558 in a Grisaugh Manor rental:

> '2 purprists (properties) in Damgate Prints corner
> Richard Brown holdeth to him and his heirs........ 2
> purprists lieng in Damgate whereof one purprist (2 and a
> half pence) lieth next the Chappell of St Thomas the Martyr
> in a certyne corner called Prints under which water
> runneth.'

There was a stone marked 'W', now under a rear extension.

The Goat Inn, Church Street, is near left

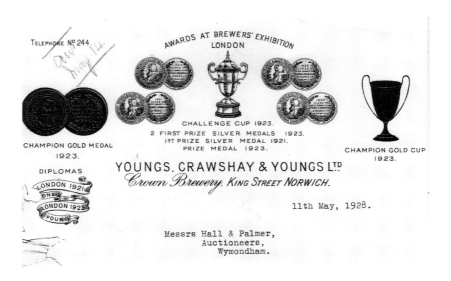

Messrs Hall & Palmer were entrusted by the Crown Brewery to sell by public auction their property, late the Goat, in May 1928.